ec 2019

DAIRY FARMERS

Elizabeth Krajnik

Published in 2020 by The Rosen Publishing Group, Inc.
29 East 21st Street, New York, NY 10010

First Edition

Editor: Greg Roza
Book Design: Reann Nye

Photo Credits: Cover Cavan Images/Cavan/Getty Images; p. 5 TonyV3112/Shutterstock.com; p. 6 SGr/Shutterstock.com; p. 7 bibiphoto/Shutterstock.com; p. 9 Chutima Chaochaiya/Shutterstock.com; p. 10 Westend61/Getty Images; p. 11 Chelle129/Shutterstock.com; p. 13 279photo Studio/Shutterstock.com; p. 14 Peopleimages/E+/Getty Images; p. 15 pixinoo/Shutterstokc.com; p. 16 Monkey Business Images/Shutterstock.com; p. 17 Bloomberg/Getty Images; p. 19 John Giustina/Photodisc/Getty Images Plus/Getty Images; p. 20 David MG/Shutterstock.com; p. 21 Ross Gordon Henry/Shutterstock.com; p. 22 gabriel12/Shutterstock.com.

Cataloging-in-Publication Data

Names: Krajnik, Elizabeth.
Title: Dairy farmers / Elizabeth Krajnik.
Description: New York : PowerKids Press, 2020. | Series: Getting the job done | Includes glossary and index.
Identifiers: ISBN 9781725301283 (pbk.) | ISBN 9781725301306 (library bound) | ISBN 9781725301290 (6pack)
Subjects: LCSH: Dairy farmers–Juvenile literature. | Dairy farming–Juvenile literature. | Dairy processing–Juvenile literature.
Classification: LCC SF239.5 K73 2020 | DDC 636.2'142–dc23

Manufactured in the United States of America

CPSIA Compliance Information: Batch #CSPK19. For Further Information contact Rosen Publishing, New York, New York at 1-800-237-9932.

CONTENTS

A PART OF EVERYDAY LIFE

Imagine you're pouring yourself a bowl of cereal. As soon as you walk to the refrigerator and grab the milk carton, you notice there's no milk left in it! Your brother or sister used the last of it. You'll need to ask your parent or guardian to get more at the store.

You have dairy farmers to thank for all things dairy: cheese, sour cream, milk, and ice cream to name a few. But these hardworking people do more than milk cows. Read on to see what it takes to be a dairy farmer. Do you think you're ready for the **challenge**?

Fascinating Career Facts

Humans began **domesticating** wild cattle about 10,500 years ago. Since then, humans have used cattle for meat and milk, for their hides, and to pull heavy loads.

Holstein cows are the most common breed, or kind, of cow used for milk **production**. Holsteins produce more milk than other breeds of dairy cows.

EARLY TO RISE

One thing that's true of almost every dairy farmer is that they have to wake up very early—sometimes as early as 3 a.m.! Milking may take several hours depending on how many head of cattle need to be milked.

Mastitis is when a cow's udder is swollen and red. A cow with mastitis can make a whole batch of milk bad. This milk has to be thrown out.

Before the farmer or farm worker can begin milking, they have to clean and dry the cow's **teats**. Then they collect a few squirts of milk into a cup to see if there are any flakes or clots, which mean the cow has mastitis. The farmer then puts a milking machine onto the cow's teats. The machine stays on for about five to seven minutes.

BREAKFAST TIME

After the cows have been milked, the farmer needs to feed them and give them plenty of fresh water. Cows that are producing milk eat about 100 pounds (45 kg) of feed a day. Dairy cow feed is a mixture of hay, grain, special corn called silage, and other things such as **vitamins** and **minerals**. All of these things are mixed and then fed to the cows.

Some dairy farms choose to grow some or all of their own feed. This means they have to grow crops in addition to caring for their cows. That's a lot of work!

Fascinating Career Facts

Farmers work closely with **nutritionists** to make sure cows are being fed the right food and getting the right **nutrients**. Healthy cows make more milk!

Many cows get most of their food from feed, while other cows get most of their food from grazing in **pastures**.

9

CARING FOR CALVES

Have you seen the tiny white hutches near farms? These shelters are where calves live. Calves are separated from their mothers shortly after they're born. This is done to protect the calf from illnesses. They're fed their mother's first milk, called colostrum. It has special **antibodies** to help protect the calf from illness and help the calf get stronger.

Separating the calf from its mother is called weaning. Some calves are only partially weaned. Those calves spend part of the day with their mother.

Dairy farmers need to keep a close eye on calves. Calves are given bottles of warm milk and a special type of feed several times a day. Calves also need fresh water and fresh hay for bedding to keep warm.

HERE COMES THE MILK TRUCK!

When cows are milked, the milk is collected and stored in large containers. The milk is stored at 39°Fahrenheit (3.8°Celsius) or colder for between 24 to 48 hours. The milk is stirred and moved around to keep it cold and to keep the milkfat from separating from the milk.

A milk truck comes to the farm about every 24 to 48 hours. These trucks have special tanks to keep the milk cold while it's being **transported** from the farm to the factory where it is **processed**. After the milk is collected and before cows are milked again, the farmer cleans the milk collection containers.

Fascinating Career Facts

Before milk is collected, the milk truck driver takes a sample of the milk and grades it. If the milk fails grading, the driver won't collect it.

Milk is tested again when it reaches the processing plant. If the milk is approved, it is pumped into storage containers and is processed.

13

CHECKING ON THE GIRLS

Dairy farmers need to check on their cows throughout the day. If the cows spend their day inside the barn, their feed may need to be moved or their droppings may need to be scooped away and the floors of the barn may need to be cleaned. If the cows spend most of their day in the pasture, they may need to be moved to a different part so they have enough grass or hay to graze on.

On large farms, cows may spend much of the day in the barn. Most barns are free stall, which means cows can choose which stall to lie in. Cows spend about 12 to 14 hours a day lying down.

Dairy farmers also take note of which cows are active and which are not. Cows that aren't very active may be sick and the farmer may need to call a veterinarian.

A VISIT FROM THE VET

Cows, just like people, can get sick. If a farmer thinks one of their cows is sick, they'll need to call the vet. Luckily, farmers and vets work together closely. Dairy vets not only treat sick cows but also work hard to keep cows from getting sick in the first place.

Fascinating Career Facts

Some dairy farms employ their own veterinarians. Dairy veterinarians pay close attention to things such as the weather, what the cows are eating, and what they're droppings are like.

If a cow gets sick and needs **antibiotics**, she may be separated from the other cows and her milk is thrown away. Milk that has antibiotics in it can't be sold. Vets also do checkups to make sure the cows are healthy and happy.

SECOND MILKING

Milking cows keep producing milk all day, which means they must be milked at least two times a day. If they aren't, their udders become too full and may be painful for the cow. Some farmers even choose to milk their cows three times a day.

Some dairy farms are family owned. This means that the farmer's children often learn to help with milking the cows from an early age. If someone's family doesn't own a farm, they can start their career as a farmhand and later become a manager or supervisor. A college degree is required, but a manager can earn more than $60,000 a year.

Some children take part in 4-H youth groups and raise cows to show at fairs and then sell them. This is a great way for kids to learn what it takes to keep a farm running.

19

PREGNANCY AND CALVING

Before a cow has a calf, it is called a heifer. Heifers don't produce milk. Cows only produce milk after they have had a calf. To keep producing milk, dairy cows must give birth to one calf per year. Heifers are old enough to have a calf at around two to three years old. Heifers and dry cows, which are cows that have previously had a calf, are pregnant for about 283 days.

Fascinating Career Facts

When they're about six years old, dairy cows are culled. This means they are sold for their meat and hides.

Cows having a calf are often put in separate pens in the months leading up to when they give birth. This is to make sure the cow has a safe, dry, clean place to give birth.

Around 10 months after calving, a cow's milk production decreases. To prevent this from happening, the cow will get pregnant again about two to three months after calving.

GETTING DIRTY

Being a dairy farmer is a hard job and it's rarely ever clean. Dairy farmers have to deal with cow droppings and even blood sometimes. However, they need to get dirty to do their job well. Dairy farmers will likely always have some part of their work that requires them to get dirty. But the job is changing.

The future of dairy farming is here. Robots are already milking cows at some farms. In some cases, farmers don't even touch an udder or round up the cows with the help of a dog. Robots do that, too!

As a dirty and changing job, do you have what it takes to be a dairy farmer?

GLOSSARY

antibiotic: A drug that is used to kill harmful bacteria and to cure infections.

antibody: A substance produced by the body to fight disease.

challenge: Something that is hard to do.

domesticate: To breed and raise an animal for use by people.

mineral: A naturally occurring solid substance that is not of plant or animal origin.

nutrient: Something taken in by a plant or animal that helps it grow and stay healthy.

nutritionist: A person whose job is to give advice on how food affects the health of people or animals.

pasture: Land on which animals graze.

process: To change something from one form into another.

production: The process of making something.

teat: The part of a female animal, such as a cow, through which a young animal receives milk.

transport: To carry from one place to another.

vaccine: A substance that is generally given to a person or animal to protect against a particular disease.

vitamin: A natural substance that is generally found in foods that helps your body to be healthy.

INDEX

WEBSITES

Due to the changing nature of Internet links, PowerKids Press has developed an online list of websites related to the subject of this book. This site is updated regularly. Please use this link to access the list: www.powerkidslinks.com/GTJD/dairy